Planner

July 2021 – June 2022

2021

JANUARY
S	M	T	W	T	F	S
					1	2
3	4	5	6	7	8	9
10	11	12	13	14	15	16
17	18	19	20	21	22	23
24	25	26	27	28	29	30
31						

FEBRUARY
S	M	T	W	T	F	S
	1	2	3	4	5	6
7	8	9	10	11	12	13
14	15	16	17	18	19	20
21	22	23	24	25	26	27
28						

MARCH
S	M	T	W	T	F	S
	1	2	3	4	5	6
7	8	9	10	11	12	13
14	15	16	17	18	19	20
21	22	23	24	25	26	27
28	29	30	31			

APRIL
S	M	T	W	T	F	S
				1	2	3
4	5	6	7	8	9	10
11	12	13	14	15	16	17
18	19	20	21	22	23	24
25	26	27	28	29	30	

MAY
S	M	T	W	T	F	S
						1
2	3	4	5	6	7	8
9	10	11	12	13	14	15
16	17	18	19	20	21	22
23	24	25	26	27	28	29
30	31					

JUNE
S	M	T	W	T	F	S
		1	2	3	4	5
6	7	8	9	10	11	12
13	14	15	16	17	18	19
20	21	22	23	24	25	26
27	28	29	30			

JULY
S	M	T	W	T	F	S
				1	2	3
4	5	6	7	8	9	10
11	12	13	14	15	16	17
18	19	20	21	22	23	24
25	26	27	28	29	30	31

AUGUST
S	M	T	W	T	F	S
1	2	3	4	5	6	7
8	9	10	11	12	13	14
15	16	17	18	19	20	21
22	23	24	25	26	27	28
29	30	31				

SEPTEMBER
S	M	T	W	T	F	S
			1	2	3	4
5	6	7	8	9	10	11
12	13	14	15	16	17	18
19	20	21	22	23	24	25
26	27	28	29	30		

OCTOBER
S	M	T	W	T	F	S
					1	2
3	4	5	6	7	8	9
10	11	12	13	14	15	16
17	18	19	20	21	22	23
24	25	26	27	28	29	30
31						

NOVEMBER
S	M	T	W	T	F	S
	1	2	3	4	5	6
7	8	9	10	11	12	13
14	15	16	17	18	19	20
21	22	23	24	25	26	27
28	29	30				

DECEMBER
S	M	T	W	T	F	S
			1	2	3	4
5	6	7	8	9	10	11
12	13	14	15	16	17	18
19	20	21	22	23	24	25
26	27	28	29	30	31	

2022

JANUARY
S	M	T	W	T	F	S
						1
2	3	4	5	6	7	8
9	10	11	12	13	14	15
16	17	18	19	20	21	22
23	24	25	26	27	28	29
30	31					

FEBRUARY
S	M	T	W	T	F	S
		1	2	3	4	5
6	7	8	9	10	11	12
13	14	15	16	17	18	19
20	21	22	23	24	25	26
27	28					

MARCH
S	M	T	W	T	F	S
		1	2	3	4	5
6	7	8	9	10	11	12
13	14	15	16	17	18	19
20	21	22	23	24	25	26
27	28	29	30	31		

APRIL
S	M	T	W	T	F	S
					1	2
3	4	5	6	7	8	9
10	11	12	13	14	15	16
17	18	19	20	21	22	23
24	25	26	27	28	29	30

MAY
S	M	T	W	T	F	S
1	2	3	4	5	6	7
8	9	10	11	12	13	14
15	16	17	18	19	20	21
22	23	24	25	26	27	28
29	30	31				

JUNE
S	M	T	W	T	F	S
			1	2	3	4
5	6	7	8	9	10	11
12	13	14	15	16	17	18
19	20	21	22	23	24	25
26	27	28	29	30		

JULY
S	M	T	W	T	F	S
					1	2
3	4	5	6	7	8	9
10	11	12	13	14	15	16
17	18	19	20	21	22	23
24	25	26	27	28	29	30
31						

AUGUST
S	M	T	W	T	F	S
	1	2	3	4	5	6
7	8	9	10	11	12	13
14	15	16	17	18	19	20
21	22	23	24	25	26	27
28	29	30	31			

SEPTEMBER
S	M	T	W	T	F	S
				1	2	3
4	5	6	7	8	9	10
11	12	13	14	15	16	17
18	19	20	21	22	23	24
25	26	27	28	29	30	

OCTOBER
S	M	T	W	T	F	S
						1
2	3	4	5	6	7	8
9	10	11	12	13	14	15
16	17	18	19	20	21	22
23	24	25	26	27	28	29
30	31					

NOVEMBER
S	M	T	W	T	F	S
		1	2	3	4	5
6	7	8	9	10	11	12
13	14	15	16	17	18	19
20	21	22	23	24	25	26
27	28	29	30			

DECEMBER
S	M	T	W	T	F	S
				1	2	3
4	5	6	7	8	9	10
11	12	13	14	15	16	17
18	19	20	21	22	23	24
25	26	27	28	29	30	31

July
2021

SUNDAY	MONDAY	TUESDAY	WEDNESDAY	THURSDAY
				1 Canada Day (CAN)
4 Independence Day	5	6	7	8
11	12	13	14	15
18	19	20 Eid al-Adha	21	22
25	26	27	28	29

MONTHLY GOALS

FRIDAY	SATURDAY
2	3
9	10
16	17
23	24
Full Moon	
30	31

TOP TASKS:

HIGHLIGHTS:

THIS & THAT:

August

2021

SUNDAY	MONDAY	TUESDAY	WEDNESDAY	THURSDAY
1	2	3	4	5
	Civic Holiday (CAN)			
8	9	10	11	12
15	16	17	18	19
22	23	24	25	26
Full Moon				
29	30	31		

MONTHLY GOALS

FRIDAY	SATURDAY
6	7
13	14
20	21
27	28

TOP TASKS:

HIGHLIGHTS:

THIS & THAT:

September
2021

SUNDAY	MONDAY	TUESDAY	WEDNESDAY	THURSDAY
			1	2
5	6 Labor Day	7 Rosh Hashanah	8	9
12	13	14	15	16 Yom Kippur
19	20 Full Moon	21 First Day of Sukkot	22 Fall Begins	23
26	27	28	29	30

MONTHLY GOALS

FRIDAY	SATURDAY
3	4
10	11
	Patriot Day
17	18
24	25

TOP TASKS:

-
-
-
-
-
-
-

HIGHLIGHTS:

THIS & THAT:

October
2021

SUNDAY	MONDAY	TUESDAY	WEDNESDAY	THURSDAY
3	4	5	6	7
10	11 Columbus Day; Thanksgiving Day (CAN)	12	13	14
17	18	19	20 Full Moon	21
24	25	26	27	28
31 Halloween				

MONTHLY GOALS

FRIDAY	SATURDAY
1	2
8	9
15	16
22	23
29	30

TOP TASKS:

HIGHLIGHTS:

THIS & THAT:

November

2021

SUNDAY	MONDAY	TUESDAY	WEDNESDAY	THURSDAY
	1 All Saints' Day	2 All Souls' Day	3	4
7 Daylight Saving Time Ends	8	9	10	11 Veterans Day
14	15	16	17	18
21	22	23	24	25 Thanksgiving Day
28	29 First Day of Hanukkah	30		

MONTHLY GOALS

FRIDAY	SATURDAY
5	6
12	13
19	20
Full Moon	
26	27

TOP TASKS:

HIGHLIGHTS:

THIS & THAT:

2021
December

SUNDAY	MONDAY	TUESDAY	WEDNESDAY	THURSDAY
			1	2
5	6	7	8	9
12	13	14	15	16
19	20	21 Winter Begins	22	23
26 Kwanzaa; Boxing Day (CAN)	27	28	29	30

MONTHLY GOALS

FRIDAY	SATURDAY
3	4
10	11
17	18
	Full Moon
24	25
Christmas Eve	Christmas Day
31	
New Year's Eve	

TOP TASKS:

HIGHLIGHTS:

THIS & THAT:

January

2022

SUNDAY	MONDAY	TUESDAY	WEDNESDAY	THURSDAY
2	3	4	5	6 Epiphany
9	10	11	12	13
16	17 Martin Luther King Jr. Day; Full Moon	18	19	20
23	24	25	26	27
30	31			

MONTHLY GOALS

FRIDAY	SATURDAY
	1
	New Year's Day
7	8
14	15
21	22
28	29

TOP TASKS:

HIGHLIGHTS:

THIS & THAT:

February
2022

SUNDAY	MONDAY	TUESDAY	WEDNESDAY	THURSDAY
		1 Chinese New Year – Tiger	2 Groundhog Day	3
6	7	8	9	10
13	14 Valentine's Day	15	16 Full Moon	17
20	21 Presidents' Day	22	23	24
27	28			

MONTHLY GOALS

FRIDAY	SATURDAY
4	5
11	12
18	19
25	26

TOP TASKS:

HIGHLIGHTS:

THIS & THAT:

2022
March

SUNDAY	MONDAY	TUESDAY	WEDNESDAY	THURSDAY
		1	2	3
			Ash Wednesday	
6	7	8	9	10
13	14	15	16	17
Daylight Saving Time Begins				Purim; St. Patrick's Day
20	21	22	23	24
Spring Begins				
27	28	29	30	31

MONTHLY GOALS

FRIDAY	SATURDAY
4	5
11	12
18	19
Full Moon	
25	26

TOP TASKS:

HIGHLIGHTS:

THIS & THAT:

April

2022

SUNDAY	MONDAY	TUESDAY	WEDNESDAY	THURSDAY
3 First Day of Ramadan	4	5	6	7
10 Palm Sunday	11	12	13	14
17 Easter	18	19	20	21
24	25	26	27	28

MONTHLY GOALS

FRIDAY	SATURDAY
1 April Fool's Day	**2**
8	**9**
15 Good Friday	**16** First Day of Passover; Full Moon
22 Earth Day	**23**
29	**30**

TOP TASKS:

HIGHLIGHTS:

THIS & THAT:

May
2022

SUNDAY	MONDAY	TUESDAY	WEDNESDAY	THURSDAY
1	2	3	4	5
		Eid al-Fitr		
8	9	10	11	12
Mother's Day				
15	16	17	18	19
	Full Moon			
22	23	24	25	26
	Victoria Day (CAN)			
29	30	31		
	Memorial Day			

MONTHLY GOALS

FRIDAY	SATURDAY
6	7
13	14
20	21
	Armed Forces Day
27	28

TOP TASKS:

HIGHLIGHTS:

THIS & THAT:

2022
June

SUNDAY	MONDAY	TUESDAY	WEDNESDAY	THURSDAY
			1	2
5	6	7	8	9
12	13	14 Flag Day; Full Moon	15	16
19 Father's Day; Juneteenth	20	21 Summer Begins	22	23
26	27	28	29	30

MONTHLY GOALS

FRIDAY	SATURDAY
3	4
10	11
17	18
24	25

TOP TASKS:

HIGHLIGHTS:

THIS & THAT:

June & July

2021

MONDAY	28	TUESDAY	29	WEDNESDAY	30

WEEKLY GOALS:

THURSDAY 1
Canada Day (CAN)

FRIDAY 2

SATURDAY 3

JUL

SUNDAY 4
Independence Day

July
2021

MONDAY	5	TUESDAY	6	WEDNESDAY	7

WEEKLY GOALS:

DAILY HABIT TRACKER:	M	T	W	T	F	S	S

THURSDAY 8

FRIDAY 9

SATURDAY 10

SUNDAY 11

July
2021

MONDAY 12	TUESDAY 13	WEDNESDAY 14

WEEKLY GOALS:

THURSDAY 15

FRIDAY 16

SATURDAY 17

JUL

SUNDAY 18

July
2021

MONDAY 19

TUESDAY 20

Eid al-Adha

WEDNESDAY 21

WEEKLY GOALS:

DAILY HABIT TRACKER:	M	T	W	T	F	S	S

THURSDAY 22

FRIDAY 23

Full Moon

SATURDAY 24

SUNDAY 25

July & August

2021

MONDAY 26	TUESDAY 27	WEDNESDAY 28

WEEKLY GOALS:

DAILY HABIT TRACKER:	M	T	W	T	F	S	S

THURSDAY 29

FRIDAY 30

SATURDAY 31

JUL

AUG

SUNDAY 1

August
2021

MONDAY 2

Civic Holiday (CAN)

TUESDAY 3

WEDNESDAY 4

WEEKLY GOALS:

DAILY HABIT TRACKER: | M | T | W | T | F | S | S |
| --- | --- | --- | --- | --- | --- | --- |
| | | | | | | |
| | | | | | | |
| | | | | | | |
| | | | | | | |

THURSDAY 5

FRIDAY 6

SATURDAY 7

AUG

SUNDAY 8

August
2021

AUG

MONDAY 9	TUESDAY 10	WEDNESDAY 11

WEEKLY GOALS:

DAILY HABIT TRACKER:	M	T	W	T	F	S	S

THURSDAY 12

FRIDAY 13

SATURDAY 14

AUG

SUNDAY 15

August

2021

MONDAY	16	TUESDAY	17	WEDNESDAY	18

AUG

WEEKLY GOALS:

DAILY HABIT TRACKER:	M	T	W	T	F	S	S

THURSDAY 19

FRIDAY 20

SATURDAY 21

SUNDAY 22

Full Moon

August
2021

AUG

MONDAY	23

TUESDAY	24

WEDNESDAY	25

WEEKLY GOALS:

AUG

THURSDAY 26

FRIDAY 27

SATURDAY 28

SUNDAY 29

Aug. & Sep.
2021

MONDAY 30	TUESDAY 31	WEDNESDAY 1

WEEKLY GOALS:

DAILY HABIT TRACKER:	M	T	W	T	F	S	S

THURSDAY 2

FRIDAY 3

SATURDAY 4

SUNDAY 5

September
2021

MONDAY 6	TUESDAY 7	WEDNESDAY 8
Labor Day	Rosh Hashanah	

WEEKLY GOALS:

THURSDAY 9

FRIDAY 10

SATURDAY 11

Patriot Day

SUNDAY 12

September
2021

MONDAY 13	TUESDAY 14	WEDNESDAY 15

WEEKLY GOALS:

DAILY HABIT TRACKER:	M	T	W	T	F	S	S

THURSDAY 16

Yom Kippur

FRIDAY 17

SATURDAY 18

SUNDAY 19

SEP

September
2021

MONDAY 20	TUESDAY 21	WEDNESDAY 22
Full Moon	First Day of Sukkot	Fall Begins

WEEKLY GOALS:

DAILY HABIT TRACKER:	M	T	W	T	F	S	S

THURSDAY 23

FRIDAY 24

SATURDAY 25

SEP

SUNDAY 26

tfpublishing.com

Sep. & Oct.
2021

MONDAY 27	TUESDAY 28	WEDNESDAY 29

DAILY HABIT TRACKER:	M	T	W	T	F	S	S

THURSDAY 30

FRIDAY 1

SATURDAY 2

SUNDAY 3

SEP

OCT

October 2021

OCT

MONDAY 4	TUESDAY 5	WEDNESDAY 6

WEEKLY GOALS:

THURSDAY 7

FRIDAY 8

SATURDAY 9

OCT

SUNDAY 10

OCT

MONDAY 11	TUESDAY 12	WEDNESDAY 13
Columbus Day; Thanksgiving Day (CAN)		

WEEKLY GOALS:

THURSDAY 14

FRIDAY 15

SATURDAY 16

OCT

SUNDAY 17

October 2021

MONDAY 18	TUESDAY 19	WEDNESDAY 20
		Full Moon

WEEKLY GOALS:

DAILY HABIT TRACKER:	M	T	W	T	F	S	S

THURSDAY 21

FRIDAY 22

SATURDAY 23

SUNDAY 24

October
2021

MONDAY 25	TUESDAY 26	WEDNESDAY 27

OCT

WEEKLY GOALS:

THURSDAY 28

FRIDAY 29

SATURDAY 30

OCT

SUNDAY 31
Halloween

2021
November

NOV

MONDAY 1
All Saints' Day

TUESDAY 2
All Souls' Day

WEDNESDAY 3

WEEKLY GOALS:

THURSDAY 4

FRIDAY 5

SATURDAY 6

NOV

SUNDAY 7
Daylight Saving Time Ends

NOV

MONDAY 8	TUESDAY 9	WEDNESDAY 10

WEEKLY GOALS:

DAILY HABIT TRACKER:	M	T	W	T	F	S	S

THURSDAY 11
Veterans Day

FRIDAY 12

SATURDAY 13

SUNDAY 14

2021 November

NOV

MONDAY 15

TUESDAY 16

WEDNESDAY 17

WEEKLY GOALS:

THURSDAY 18

FRIDAY 19

Full Moon

SATURDAY 20

NOV

SUNDAY 21

November

MONDAY 22	TUESDAY 23	WEDNESDAY 24

WEEKLY GOALS:

THURSDAY 25
Thanksgiving Day

FRIDAY 26

SATURDAY 27

NOV

SUNDAY 28

Nov. & Dec.
2021

MONDAY 29

First Day of Hanukkah

TUESDAY 30

WEDNESDAY 1

WEEKLY GOALS:

	M	T	W	T	F	S	S

THURSDAY 2

FRIDAY 3

SATURDAY 4

SUNDAY 5

DEC

MONDAY 6	TUESDAY 7	WEDNESDAY 8

DEC

WEEKLY GOALS:

DAILY HABIT TRACKER:	M	T	W	T	F	S	S

THURSDAY 9

FRIDAY 10

SATURDAY 11

DEC

SUNDAY 12

2021
December

DEC

MONDAY 13

TUESDAY 14

WEDNESDAY 15

WEEKLY GOALS:

DAILY HABIT TRACKER:	M	T	W	T	F	S	S

THURSDAY 16

FRIDAY 17

SATURDAY 18

Full Moon

SUNDAY 19

DEC

2021 December

DEC

MONDAY 20

TUESDAY 21

Winter Begins

WEDNESDAY 22

WEEKLY GOALS:

	M	T	W	T	F	S	S

THURSDAY 23

FRIDAY 24

Christmas Eve

SATURDAY 25

Christmas Day

SUNDAY 26

Kwanzaa; Boxing Day (CAN)

DEC

2021 Dec. & 2022 Jan.

DEC

MONDAY 27	TUESDAY 28	WEDNESDAY 29

WEEKLY GOALS:

DAILY HABIT TRACKER:

	M	T	W	T	F	S	S

THURSDAY 30

FRIDAY 31

New Year's Eve

SATURDAY 1

New Year's Day

SUNDAY 2

DEC

JAN

January

2022

MONDAY 3	TUESDAY 4	WEDNESDAY 5

WEEKLY GOALS:

DAILY HABIT TRACKER: | M | T | W | T | F | S | S |
|---|---|---|---|---|---|---|

THURSDAY 6
Epiphany

FRIDAY 7

SATURDAY 8

SUNDAY 9

January
2022

MONDAY	10	TUESDAY	11	WEDNESDAY	12

WEEKLY GOALS:

DAILY HABIT TRACKER:	M	T	W	T	F	S	S

THURSDAY 13

FRIDAY 14

SATURDAY 15

SUNDAY 16

January

2022

MONDAY 17

Martin Luther King Jr. Day; Full Moon

TUESDAY 18

WEDNESDAY 19

JAN

WEEKLY GOALS:

DAILY HABIT TRACKER:	M	T	W	T	F	S	S

THURSDAY 20

FRIDAY 21

SATURDAY 22

SUNDAY 23

JAN

January

2022

MONDAY 24	TUESDAY 25	WEDNESDAY 26

WEEKLY GOALS:

THURSDAY 27

FRIDAY 28

SATURDAY 29

SUNDAY 30

JAN

Jan. & Feb.
2022

MONDAY 31

TUESDAY 1

Chinese New Year – Tiger

WEDNESDAY 2

Groundhog Day

JAN

FEB

WEEKLY GOALS:

THURSDAY 3

FRIDAY 4

SATURDAY 5

SUNDAY 6

FEB

February

2022

MONDAY 7	TUESDAY 8	WEDNESDAY 9

WEEKLY GOALS:

DAILY HABIT TRACKER:	M	T	W	T	F	S	S

THURSDAY 10

FRIDAY 11

SATURDAY 12

SUNDAY 13

February

2022

MONDAY 14	TUESDAY 15	WEDNESDAY 16
Valentine's Day		Full Moon

FEB

WEEKLY GOALS:

THURSDAY 17

FRIDAY 18

SATURDAY 19

SUNDAY 20

FEB

February
2022

MONDAY 21	TUESDAY 22	WEDNESDAY 23
Presidents' Day		

FEB

WEEKLY GOALS:

DAILY HABIT TRACKER:	M	T	W	T	F	S	S

THURSDAY 24

FRIDAY 25

SATURDAY 26

SUNDAY 27

FEB

Feb. & March

2022

MONDAY 28	TUESDAY 1	WEDNESDAY 2
		Ash Wednesday

FEB

MAR

WEEKLY GOALS:

THURSDAY 3

FRIDAY 4

SATURDAY 5

SUNDAY 6

MAR

MONDAY 7	TUESDAY 8	WEDNESDAY 9

WEEKLY GOALS:

DAILY HABIT TRACKER:	M	T	W	T	F	S	S

THURSDAY 10

FRIDAY 11

SATURDAY 12

SUNDAY 13
Daylight Saving Time Begins

MAR

2022
March

MONDAY 14

TUESDAY 15

WEDNESDAY 16

MAR

WEEKLY GOALS:

DAILY HABIT TRACKER:	M	T	W	T	F	S	S

THURSDAY 17
Purim; St. Patrick's Day

FRIDAY 18
Full Moon

SATURDAY 19

SUNDAY 20
Spring Begins

MONDAY 21

TUESDAY 22

WEDNESDAY 23

MAR

WEEKLY GOALS:

	M	T	W	T	F	S	S

THURSDAY 24

FRIDAY 25

SATURDAY 26

SUNDAY 27

MAR

March & April

2022

MONDAY 28	TUESDAY 29	WEDNESDAY 30

WEEKLY GOALS:

THURSDAY 31

FRIDAY 1
April Fool's Day

SATURDAY 2

SUNDAY 3
First Day of Ramadan

MAR

APR

MONDAY 4	TUESDAY 5	WEDNESDAY 6

APR

WEEKLY GOALS:

DAILY HABIT TRACKER:

	M	T	W	T	F	S	S

THURSDAY 7

FRIDAY 8

SATURDAY 9

SUNDAY 10

Palm Sunday

APR

April

MONDAY 11	TUESDAY 12	WEDNESDAY 13

APR

WEEKLY GOALS:

DAILY HABIT TRACKER:	M	T	W	T	F	S	S

THURSDAY 14

FRIDAY 15

Good Friday

SATURDAY 16

First Day of Passover; Full Moon

SUNDAY 17

Easter

APR

2022
April

MONDAY 18	TUESDAY 19	WEDNESDAY 20

WEEKLY GOALS:

THURSDAY 21

FRIDAY 22

Earth Day

SATURDAY 23

SUNDAY 24

April & May

2022

MONDAY	25

TUESDAY	26

WEDNESDAY	27

WEEKLY GOALS:

DAILY HABIT TRACKER: | M | T | W | T | F | S | S |
|---|---|---|---|---|---|---|
| | | | | | | |
| | | | | | | |
| | | | | | | |
| | | | | | | |

THURSDAY 28

FRIDAY 29

SATURDAY 30

SUNDAY 1

May
2022

MONDAY 2	TUESDAY 3	WEDNESDAY 4
	Eid al-Fitr	

WEEKLY GOALS:

THURSDAY 5

FRIDAY 6

SATURDAY 7

SUNDAY 8
Mother's Day

MAY

May
2022

MONDAY 9	TUESDAY 10	WEDNESDAY 11

WEEKLY GOALS:

DAILY HABIT TRACKER: | M | T | W | T | F | S | S |
|---|---|---|---|---|---|---|
| | | | | | | |
| | | | | | | |
| | | | | | | |
| | | | | | | |

THURSDAY 12

FRIDAY 13

SATURDAY 14

SUNDAY 15

May

2022

MONDAY 16	TUESDAY 17	WEDNESDAY 18
Full Moon		

WEEKLY GOALS:

THURSDAY 19

FRIDAY 20

SATURDAY 21

Armed Forces Day

SUNDAY 22

May
2022

MONDAY 23	TUESDAY 24	WEDNESDAY 25
Victoria Day (CAN)		

WEEKLY GOALS:

DAILY HABIT TRACKER:	M	T	W	T	F	S	S

THURSDAY 26

FRIDAY 27

SATURDAY 28

SUNDAY 29

May & June

2022

MONDAY 30	TUESDAY 31	WEDNESDAY 1
Memorial Day		

WEEKLY GOALS:

DAILY HABIT TRACKER:	M	T	W	T	F	S	S

THURSDAY 2

FRIDAY 3

SATURDAY 4

SUNDAY 5

2022
June

| MONDAY | 6 | TUESDAY | 7 | WEDNESDAY | 8 |

WEEKLY GOALS:

DAILY HABIT TRACKER:	M	T	W	T	F	S	S

THURSDAY 9

FRIDAY 10

SATURDAY 11

SUNDAY 12

2022
June

MONDAY 13	TUESDAY 14	WEDNESDAY 15
	Flag Day; Full Moon	

WEEKLY GOALS:

THURSDAY 16

FRIDAY 17

SATURDAY 18

SUNDAY 19
Father's Day; Juneteenth

June
2022

MONDAY 20

TUESDAY 21

Summer Begins

WEDNESDAY 22

WEEKLY GOALS:

DAILY HABIT TRACKER: | M | T | W | T | F | S | S |
|---|---|---|---|---|---|---|
| | | | | | | |
| | | | | | | |
| | | | | | | |
| | | | | | | |

THURSDAY 23

FRIDAY 24

SATURDAY 25

SUNDAY 26

June & July

2022

MONDAY 27	TUESDAY 28	WEDNESDAY 29

WEEKLY GOALS:

THURSDAY 30

FRIDAY 1

Canada Day (CAN)

SATURDAY 2

SUNDAY 3

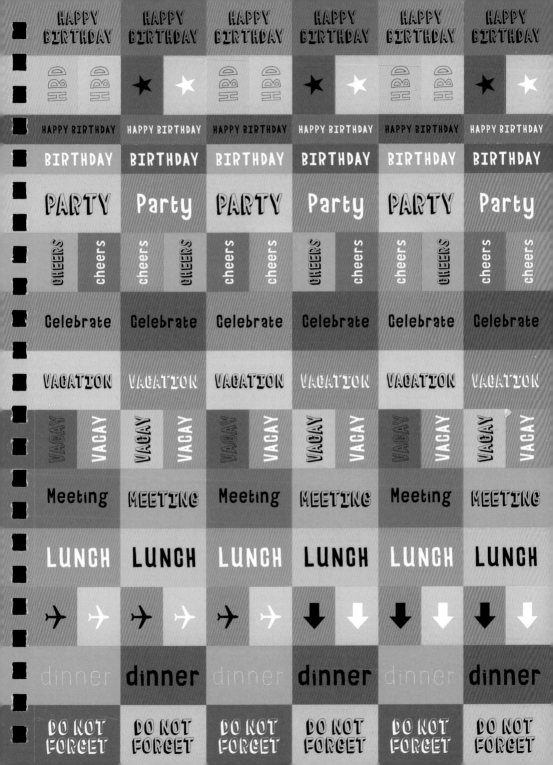

Appointment	Appointment	Appointment	Appointment	Appointment	Appointment
To Do	to do	★	☆	To Do	to do	★	☆	To Do	to do	★	☆

To Do	to do	★	☆	To Do	to do	★	☆	To Do	to do	★	☆

reminder	REMEMBER	reminder	REMEMBER	reminder	REMEMBER
REMEMBER	reminder	REMEMBER	reminder	REMEMBER	reminder
ANNIVERSARY	Anniversary	ANNIVERSARY	Anniversary	ANNIVERSARY	Anniversary

Fun	FUN	Fun	Fun	FUN	Fun	DUE	due	DUE	DUE	due	DUE

Wedding	Wedding	Wedding	Shower	Shower	Shower
Doctor	Doctor	Doctor	Doctor	important	important

$	$	$	!	!	!	⊠	⊠	⊠	☕	☕	☕

action REQUIRED	action REQUIRED	action REQUIRED	action REQUIRED	URGENT	URGENT
Game	Game	NIGHT out	HAPPY HOUR	NIGHT out	HAPPY HOUR

☺	☺	☺	☺	☺	☺	♥	♥	♥	♥	♥	♥

RSVP	RSVP	big DAY	big DAY	HAIR	HAIR
CAR service	Taxes	so very busy	so very busy	LOVE	LOVE